I0416440

August 2012

# FEDERAL COMMUNICATIONS COMMISSION

## Regulatory Fee Process Needs to Be Updated

# FEDERAL COMMUNICATIONS COMMISSION

## Regulatory Fee Process Needs to Be Updated

## Why GAO Did This Study

FCC must by law assess annual regulatory fees on telecommunications entities to recover its entire appropriation—about $336 million in fiscal year 2011. The entities from which FCC collects fees fall into one of five main industry sectors (broadcast, cable, wireline, wireless, and international) and are assigned to one of 86 fee categories, such as paging services. Recently, FCC stated that it was planning to consider reforms to its regulatory fee process. GAO was asked to examine (1) FCC's process for assessing regulatory fees among industry sectors, (2) FCC's regulatory fee collections over the past 10 years, and (3) alternative approaches to assessing regulatory fees. GAO reviewed FCC data and documents, interviewed officials from FCC and the telecommunications industry, and, to identify alternative approaches to assessing regulatory fees, met with five fee-funded U.S. and Canadian regulatory agencies.

## What GAO Recommends

Congress should consider whether FCC's excess fees should be appropriated for FCC's use or, if not, what their disposition should be. FCC should perform an updated FTE analysis and require at least biennial updates going forward; determine whether and how to revise the current fee schedule, including the number of fee categories; increase the transparency of its regulatory fee process; and consider the approaches of other fee-funded regulatory agencies. FCC agreed with GAO's recommendations.

View GAO-12-686. For more information, contact Mark L. Goldstein at (202) 512-2834 or goldsteinm@gao.gov

## What GAO Found

The Federal Communications Commission (FCC) assesses regulatory fees among industry sectors and fee categories based on obsolete data, with limited transparency. The Communications Act requires FCC to base its regulatory fees on the number of full-time equivalents (FTE) that perform regulatory tasks in certain bureaus, among other things. FCC based its fiscal year 2011 regulatory fee assessments on its fiscal year 1998 division of FTEs among fee categories. It has not updated the FTE analysis on which it bases its regulatory fees, in part to avoid fluctuations in fees from year to year. FCC officials stated that the agency has complied with its statutory authority by dividing fees among fee categories based on FTE data—although the data is from fiscal year 1998— since the statute does not prescribe a specific time for FCC to update its FTE analysis. As a result, after 13 years in a rapidly changing industry, FCC has not validated the extent to which its fees correlate to its workload. Major changes in the telecommunications industry include the increasing use of wireless and broadband services and a convergence of telecommunications industries. Moreover, FCC's practice is inconsistent with federal guidance on user fees. As a result of FCC's use of obsolete data in assessing regulatory fees, companies in some fee categories may be subsidizing companies in others. FCC officials said it has become more challenging to align current FTEs to the 86 fee categories given the increasingly cross-cutting nature of FCC's work, raising the potential that FCC's fee categories may also be out of date. FCC's regulatory fee process also lacks transparency because of the limited nature of the information FCC has published on it. This has made it difficult for industry and other stakeholders to understand and provide input on fee assessments. On July 17, 2012, FCC released a regulatory fee reform *Notice of Proposed Rulemaking (NPRM)* proposing changes to FCC's regulatory fee program related to many issues raised in this report.

On average over the past 10 years, FCC collected 2 percent more in regulatory fees than it was required to collect. Prior to fiscal year 2008, FCC's annual appropriations stated that any excess regulatory fees remained available until expended; since 2008, FCC's annual appropriations have prohibited the use of any excess fees from the current year or previous years without an appropriation by Congress. As a result, $66 million in excess fees currently resides in an account at the Department of Treasury that cannot be used without congressional action. The account has increased by an average of $6.7 million per year for fiscal years 2006 through 2011. Congress has not provided for the disposition of these accumulating excess funds.

Approaches of other fee-funded regulatory agencies could be instructive as FCC considers reforms. For example, the Nuclear Regulatory Commission, Federal Energy Regulatory Commission, and Canadian Radio-television and Telecommunications Commission assess fees based on an annually or biennially updated analysis of costs by industry sector. Regarding excess fees, officials at five other fee-funded regulatory agencies stated that their agencies either apply excess fees as an adjustment to the subsequent year's fees or refund them.

# Contents

**Abbreviations**

| | |
|---|---|
| CNCS | Canadian Nuclear Safety Commission |
| CRTC | Canadian Radio-television and Telecommunications Commission |
| FCA | Farm Credit Administration |
| FCC | Federal Communications Commission |
| FERC | Federal Energy Regulatory Commission |
| FNPRM | Further Notice of Proposed Rulemaking |
| FTE | full-time equivalent |
| ITTA | Independent Telephone and Telecommunications Alliance |
| NCTA | National Cable and Telecommunications Association |
| NPRM | Notice of Proposed Rulemaking |
| NRC | Nuclear Regulatory Commission |
| VoIP | voice over Internet protocol |
| Y2K | year 2000 |

United States Government Accountability Office
Washington, DC 20548

August 10, 2012

The Honorable Henry A. Waxman
Ranking Member
Committee on Energy and Commerce
House of Representatives

The Honorable Anna G. Eshoo
Ranking Member
Subcommittee on Communications and Technology
Committee on Energy and Commerce
House of Representatives

The Federal Communications Commission (FCC), which regulates interstate and international communications by radio, television, wire, satellite, and cable in the United States, must by law assess and collect annual regulatory fees from the entities it regulates. These fees are designed to recover FCC's operating costs, covering its enforcement, policy and rulemaking, international, and user information activities.[1] In recent appropriation acts, Congress has directed FCC to recover its entire appropriation—about $336 million for fiscal year 2011—through the collection of these regulatory fees.[2] The entities from which FCC collects fees fall into one of five main industry sectors (broadcast, cable, wireline, wireless, and international) and are assigned to 1 of 86 fee categories. FCC has referred to the process as a "zero-sum proposition" because, since FCC is directed to collect a specified amount by Congress, if FCC reduces the fees of one industry sector or fee category, others must pay

---

[1]Act of June 19, 1934, ch. 652, § 9, 48 Stat. 1064, as amended (codified at 47 U.S.C. § 159). Throughout this report, the 1934 Act as amended is referred to as the Communications Act; specific provisions are cited to the United States Code.

[2]See the Full-Year Continuing Appropriations Act, 2011, Pub. L. No. 112-10, Div. B, § 1101(a)(6), 125 Stat. 38, 103 (2011), for the appropriations act language specifying that the applicable level, authority and conditions of funding for fiscal year 2011 continued to be as provided by the Consolidated Appropriations Act, 2010, Pub. L. No. 111-117, 123 Stat. 3034, 3184-3185 (2009) for agencies previously funded by that act. The level set by Congress in the Consolidated Appropriations Act, 2010 for FCC was $335,794,000 of offsetting collections to be assessed and collected by FCC pursuant to the Communications Act.

more.[3] Recently, concerns have been raised that FCC's regulatory fee process does not align with today's communications industry and may provide a competitive advantage to some industries while disadvantaging others. In fiscal years 2008, 2011, and 2012, FCC stated that it was planning to consider reforms to its regulatory fee process, in part because the communications industry had changed dramatically since 1994 when FCC's regulatory fee process was first authorized, while FCC's division of regulatory fees among industry sectors and fee categories had changed very little.

To offset FCC's annual appropriation through regulatory fees, FCC determines how to divide the amount to be collected among the five industry sectors and fee categories within each industry sector.[4] FCC also determines a rate to charge entities within each fee category.[5] FCC sets the rates of different fee categories on various bases. For example, FCC sets the rate for wireline telephone companies on a per-revenue-dollar basis—$.00375 per revenue dollar in fiscal year 2011, for total expected collections from the industry of about $148 million.[6] On the other hand, FCC sets the rate for wireless telephone companies on a per subscriber basis[7]—$0.17 per subscriber in fiscal year 2011, for total expected collections from the industry of about $51 million. Figure 1 illustrates the process FCC uses to assess and collect regulatory fees each year.

---

[3]*In the Matter of Assessment and Collection of Regulatory Fees for fiscal year 2004,* 19 FCC Rcd. 11662, 11666 (2004).

[4]FCC refers to its process of dividing the amount to be collected among fee categories as all allocation process.

[5]Each year, FCC designates either a rate, based on revenues, subscribers, or another basis, or a flat fee for each of the 86 fee categories.

[6]What we refer to in this report as the fee category for wireline telephone companies, FCC refers to as the fee category for interstate telecommunications service providers. According to FCC, providers subject to this fee category typically identify themselves using one or more of the following descriptions: competitive access provider, competitive local exchange carrier (CLEC); incumbent local exchange provider (ILEC); interconnected voice over internet protocol (VoIP) provider; or interexchange carrier, among others. Only certain revenues of these companies are used in computing the regulatory fees they pay.

[7]FCC's fee category for wireless telephone (cell phone) providers is called the Commercial Mobile Radio Service (CMRS) fee category. In this report, we refer to this fee category as the wireless telephone fee category.

**Figure 1: FCC's Regulatory Fee Assessment Process**

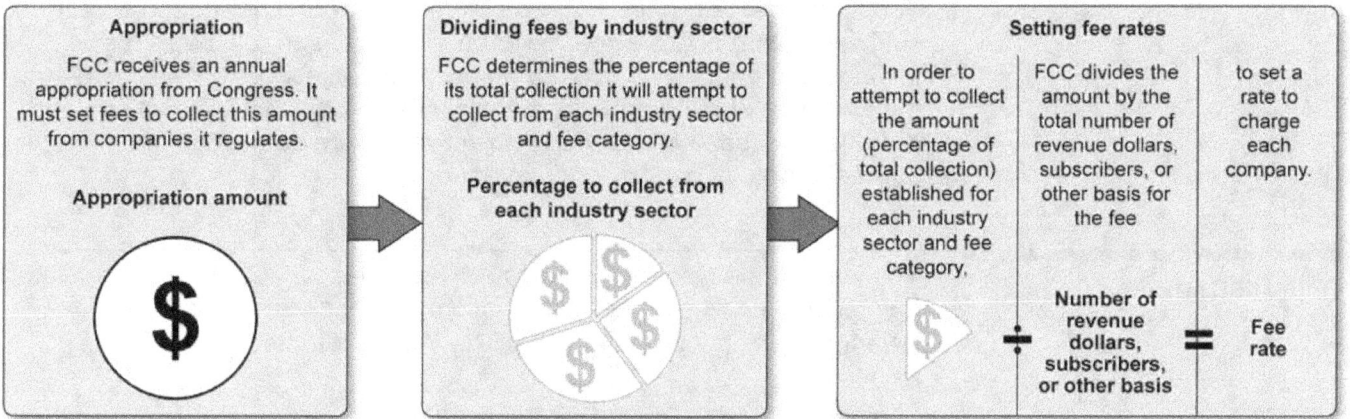

Source: GAO presentation of FCC information.

Note: In some cases, FCC charges each company within a fee category a flat fee. For example, within the media industry sector, FCC has divided broadcast television stations into 10 fee categories (5 for VHF stations and 5 for UHF stations) based on market share. Each television station within each fee category pays the same flat fee.

In response to your request that we review FCC's regulatory fee process, we reviewed (1) FCC's process for assessing regulatory fees among industry sectors and the results of this process, (2) FCC's regulatory fee collections over the past 10 years compared to the amount FCC was directed to collect by Congress, and (3) alternative approaches to assessing regulatory fees that could be instructive as FCC considers reforming its process. To examine FCC's regulatory fee process and annual regulatory fee collections, we reviewed, among other things, relevant statutes and budgetary documents, FCC documents, and FCC fee-collection data. We spoke with internal and external stakeholders, including FCC officials, media and telecommunications trade associations, and companies from each of the five main industry sectors that paid FCC regulatory fees in fiscal year 2010. To identify alternatives to FCC's current regulatory fee process, we selected, met with, and reviewed documents from five U.S. or Canadian agencies based on the criteria that they, like FCC, be independent regulatory commissions that recover the majority or all of their costs through annual fees assessed on regulated entities. The agencies included (1) Canadian Nuclear Safety Commission (CNSC), (2) Canadian Radio-television and Telecommunications Commission (CRTC), (3) Farm Credit Administration (FCA), (4) Federal Energy Regulatory Commission (FERC), and (5) Nuclear Regulatory Commission (NRC).

We conducted this performance audit from May 2011 to August 2012 in accordance with generally accepted government auditing standards. Those standards require that we plan and perform the audit to obtain sufficient, appropriate evidence to provide a reasonable basis for our findings and conclusions based on our audit objectives. We believe that the evidence obtained provides a reasonable basis for our findings and conclusions based on our audit objectives. More detailed information on our methodology can be found in appendix I.

## Background

Section 9 of the Communications Act authorizes FCC to collect regulatory fees annually.[8] These regulatory fees do not include application fees or revenue from spectrum auctions. The statute directs FCC to do the following:

- Assess and collect regulatory fees to recover the costs of FCC's regulatory activities, defined by section 9 as consisting of its enforcement, policy and rulemaking, user information, and international activities—in the amount required in FCC's appropriation acts.

- Derive these fees by determining the full-time equivalent (FTE)[9] number of employees performing these regulatory activities in three named bureaus and other FCC offices—adjusted to take into account various factors that are reasonably related to the benefits to the fee payors, including factors determined by FCC to be in the public interest. (According to FCC officials, the three bureaus named in section 9—the Private Radio, Mass Media, and Common Carrier Bureaus—have since been reorganized and renamed as the Wireless Telecommunications Bureau, the Media Bureau, the Wireline Competition Bureau, and the International Bureau.)

- Make mandatory adjustments. FCC maintains and is required annually to revise a schedule of regulatory fees to reflect

---

[8]47 U.S.C. § 159. FCC also collects application fees from companies for activities such as license applications, renewals or requests for modification. These fees are deposited in the General Fund of the Treasury and cannot be used by FCC. 47 U.S.C. § 158(e).

[9]An FTE reflects the total number of regular straight-time hours (i.e., not including overtime or holiday hours) worked by employees divided by the number of compensable hours applicable to each fiscal year. Annual leave, sick leave, and compensatory time off and other approved leave categories are considered to be "hours worked" for purposes of defining FTE employment.

proportionate increases or decreases in the amount of the appropriation to be recovered as well as changes in the number of licensees or other units required to pay the fees assessed.

- Make permitted amendments as necessary. FCC is required to amend the schedule if FCC determines that the schedule must be amended to comply with the statute's requirement that the fees be derived by determining FTEs (as outlined above), adjusted to take into account factors reasonably related to the benefits the fee payor receives from FCC regulation, among other things.

In recent years, Congress has included language in FCC's annual appropriation act setting specific percentages of the appropriation FCC is to offset with collected regulatory fees. This percentage has risen from 38 percent in 1994, when section 9 first went into effect, to over 99 percent starting in 2004, to 100 percent starting in 2009.[10] In fiscal year 2011, FCC's appropriation, and hence the total in regulatory fees it was to use as offsets, was about $336 million. According to FCC officials, this appropriation funded about 1,556 FTEs in FCC's 11 offices and 7 bureaus. The 7 bureaus include the (1) Consumer and Governmental Affairs, (2) Enforcement, (3) International, (4) Media, (5) Public Safety and Homeland Security, (6) Wireless Telecommunications, and (7) Wireline Competition Bureaus.

The five industry sectors in which FCC has typically grouped regulatory fee payors include: (1) wireline services, (2) wireless services, (3) cable services, (4) broadcast services, and (5) international services. At times, FCC has combined cable and broadcast into an industry sector it calls media—aligning the four industry sectors with four FCC bureaus—wireline with the Wireline Competition Bureau, wireless with the Wireless Telecommunications Bureau, media with the Media Bureau, and

---

[10]Departments of Commerce, Justice, and State, the Judiciary, and Related Agencies Appropriations Act, 1994, Pub. L. No. 103–121, 107 Stat 1153, 1166-1167 (1993); Omnibus Appropriations Act, 2009, Pub. L. No. 111-8, 123 Stat. 524, 657 (2009). As the appropriation acts make clear, the collected fees are treated as offsetting receipts. Unlike offsetting collections, which are available for obligation by the agency without further legislative action, offsetting receipts cannot be used without being appropriated. GAO, *A Glossary of Terms Used in the Federal Budget Process.* GAO-05-734SP (Washington, D.C.: Sept. 2005). Congress has indicated in recent FCC appropriation acts that offsetting receipts collected in a given fiscal year are not available to FCC beyond the amount initially appropriated. Fees collected in excess of the amount appropriated may not be obligated without additional congressional action.

international with the International Bureau. As shown in Table 1, within most of these industry sectors are a number of fee categories.

**Table 1: Examples of FCC Fee Categories within Each Industry Sector**

| Industry sector | Number of fee categories, fiscal year 2011 | Examples of fee categories within industry sector |
|---|---|---|
| Wireline | 1 | Wireline telephone |
| Wireless | 14 | Wireless telephone, paging, broadband radio service; and a number of fee categories considered small wireless, such as aviation aircraft, aviation ground, marine coast, and amateur vanity call signals |
| Cable/Media | 2 | Cable television systems, Cable access relay service |
| Broadcast/Media | 60 | UHF and VHF Television stations (divided into different markets), am and fm radio stations (divided into different classes and by population served) |
| International | 9 | Submarine cable (divided into 5 fee categories based on capacity); earth station satellites; international bearer circuits (terrestrial and satellite services); geostationary space stations, including direct broadcast satellite television operators; nongeostationary space stations |
| **Total for all industry sectors** | **86** | |

Source: GAO analysis of FCC information.

Each year, FCC sets a rate for each fee category that is used to calculate how much each company within that category owes in regulatory fees. FCC assesses this rate on various bases. For example, the rate for wireline telephone companies is set per revenue dollar (for those revenues subject to fees);[11] the rate for wireless telephone companies and cable television operators is based on the number of subscribers; the rate for geostationary orbit space stations, including operators of direct-broadcast satellite television, is based on the number of satellites; and broadcast television and radio licensees pay a flat fee that is set based on market reach characteristics, such as the size of the market area or population served.[12] Entities that provide services in more than one fee category—such as a company that offers wireline and wireless services—

---

[11]The wireline telephone company regulatory fee rate is based on billed interstate and international end-use revenues for local and most toll services. Other types of revenue are excluded from the regulatory fee calculation.

[12]Specifically, the fee categories for commercial television stations are based on whether the station is broadcasting on VHF or UHF frequencies and the size of the Nielsen Designated Market Area. The fee categories for commercial radio stations are based on the class of station and population served.

must pay regulatory fees for each fee category commensurate with the service provided.

Each year, FCC issues a *Notice of Proposed Rulemaking (NPRM)* in which it proposes how it will assess fees by industry sector and fee category for that fiscal year. FCC receives comments on the *NPRM* and may make adjustments before issuing a Report and Order establishing assessment rates for each year's regulatory fees. FCC also establishes a due date for payment. Entities that are late in paying their assessed fees are assessed an additional one-time 25 percent statutory penalty,[13] and FCC will take no action on any applications or other requests for benefits from such an entity until its past due assessment is paid. According to FCC officials, while the timing of this process varies somewhat from year to year, the assessment is collected in time for FCC to process payment and forward it to the Department of Treasury by the end of the fiscal year on September 30. For example, in fiscal year 2011, the *NPRM* was issued on May 3, 2011, and comments were accepted until June 9, 2011. The Report and Order was released on July 22, 2011, and the assessed fees were due on September 16, 2011.

# FCC's Assessment of Regulatory Fees Is Based on Obsolete Data and Lacks Transparency

## FCC's Regulatory Fee Assessments

From fiscal year 1998 through its most recent assessment for fiscal year 2011, FCC has based its division of regulatory fees among industry sectors and fee categories on its fiscal year 1998 division of FTEs among fee categories. FCC determined this fiscal year 1998 division of FTEs among fee categories through a cost-accounting system that FCC abandoned in fiscal year 1999 because of problems described in greater

---

[13]47 U.S.C. § 159(c)(1).

detail below.[14] In subsequent years, FCC continued to use the same basic division of fees among fee categories established in fiscal year 1998, with some adjustments to the rates of certain fee categories, based on (for example) concerns about overburdening particular industries.[15] These adjustments were not based on any FTE analysis and have had relatively minor effects on the division of regulatory fees by industry sector that FCC established in fiscal year 1998, as shown in figure 2.

[14]In a fiscal year 2008 Further Notice of Proposed Rulemaking, FCC stated that FCC's division of fees among fee categories was based on FCC's 1994 calculation of FTEs devoted to each regulatory fee category. See *In the Matter of Assessment and Collection of Regulatory Fees for Fiscal Year 2008*, 24 FCC Rcd. 6389, 6401 (2008). According to FCC officials, the 2008 FNPRM should have referred to FCC's fiscal year 1998 calculation of FTEs. FCC staff confirmed that the FTE analysis was last conducted in 1998. Since 1994, FCC has used its authority under section 9 to modify the service categories and amounts set out in the Schedule of Regulatory Fees in order to reflect changes in the number of payment units, additions and changes in the services subject to the fee requirement, and the benefits derived from FCC's activities, and to simplify the structure of the schedule. See Appendix F, "Detailed Guidance on Who Must Pay Regulatory Fees," *Assessment and Collection of Regulatory Fees for Fiscal Year 2000*, 15 FCC Rcd. 14478, 14539 (2000). FCC has continued to use FTE data compiled in fiscal year 1998 to determine the proportion of the total regulatory fees assigned to each fee category.

[15]Based on FCC-provided information, we determined that the cumulative effect of all of the adjustments made by FCC was that for fiscal year 2011, FCC expected the wireline telephone industry to pay about $8.6 million less than it would have paid had FCC based fees only on the division established by its fiscal year 1998 FTE analysis. In turn, FCC expected the other industry sectors to pay more ($2.1 million more for the wireless industry; $3.4 million more for the cable industry, $2.6 million more for the media industry, and $1.2 million more for the international industry).

**Figure 2: FCC's Division of Regulatory Fees among Industry Sectors, Fiscal Years 1998 and 2011**

Fiscal year 1998, FCC directed to collect $163 million          Fiscal year 2011, FCC directed to collect $336 million

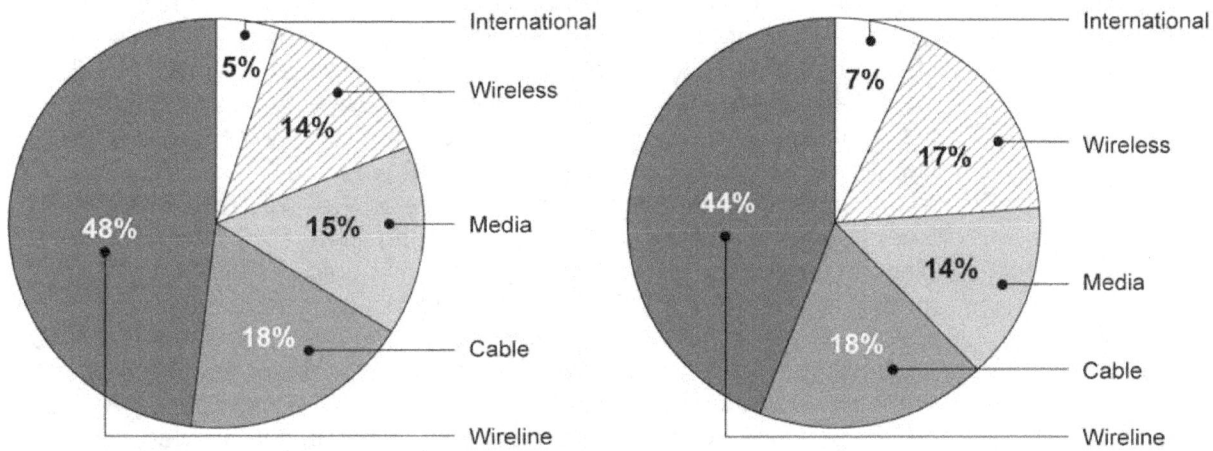

Source: GAO analysis of FCC data.

## Statutory Framework

In fiscal year 1994, when FCC first implemented the Communications Act regulatory fee statute, FCC used the fee schedule Congress had included as a starting point in the statute. That schedule, which was developed based on information provided to Congress by FCC, set annual regulatory fees for 46 fee categories that FCC was to follow until FCC amended the schedule.[16] The fee schedule established numerous fee categories—46— assessed on different bases, including a flat fee basis, a per subscriber basis, a per antenna basis, and others. While FCC has made changes to this fee schedule over the years, including adding and altering fee categories, the basic elements of its structure—established based on the telecommunications industry as it existed in 1994, and in the context of directing FCC to collect fees to cover 38 percent of its appropriation

---

[16]In 1991, the House of Representatives, in a bill that would have established FCC's authority to charge regulatory fees, adopted a proposed annual fee schedule that was informed by information provided by FCC on how FCC allocated its costs among bureaus and service categories. The legislation did not become law in 1991. However, the fee provisions that became law in 1993 were virtually identical to those in the 1991 bill, with the exception of the level of the fees themselves. See H.R. Rep. 102-207, 102nd Cong. (1991).

instead of the 100 percent that FCC has been directed to collect since fiscal year 2009—have continued to guide FCC's regulatory fee assessment.

The Communications Act requires FCC to develop accounting systems necessary for the agency to determine whether and how the fee schedule should be adjusted to comply with the statute's requirement that FCC base its regulatory fees on the number of FTEs performing regulatory tasks, among other things.[17] The act does not specify that the system should be a *cost* accounting system—FCC was free to interpret this requirement according to its perceived needs. Nevertheless, in its Reports and Orders for the 2 years following 1994, FCC discussed its plans to develop a cost-accounting system to guide its division of fees among fee categories. FCC implemented this cost-accounting system, which relied on employees' coding of time and attendance report entries, for fiscal years 1997 and 1998, using it as the basis for dividing fees among fee categories. At the time, FCC stated that its purpose in using a cost-accounting system based on employees' time card entries was to ensure that fee collections from each category of service approximated, to the extent possible, FCC's actual costs to regulate each fee category.[18]

FCC abandoned the use of this system to track costs according to fee category after fiscal year 1998 because the agency found use of the system to be problematic.[19] Specifically, according to FCC officials, basing its division of fees on employees' time card entries caused too

---

[17] As previously stated, FCC is required to base its regulatory fees on the number of FTEs performing regulatory tasks in three named bureaus plus other FCC offices, as adjusted to take into account factors that are reasonably related to the benefits provided by FCC's activities to those entities paying the fee, including factors determined by FCC to be in the public interest.

[18] This system, as described in the 1997 Report and Order, was in line with federal cost accounting guidance in that it identified direct costs, such as payroll and other direct costs, and assigned these costs to fee categories via program codes recorded by employees on their time sheets in what appeared to be a rational and systematic manner. In addition, it allocated other indirect costs pro-rata to direct costs and distributed overhead costs based on predetermined allocation formulas. However, as the system is no longer in use, we were unable to validate the extent to which it met federal cost accounting standards. See *In the Matter of Assessment and Collection of Regulatory Fees for Fiscal Year 1997*, 12 FCC Rcd. (1997).

[19] *In the Matter of Assessment and Collection of Regulatory Fees for Fiscal Year 2004*, 19 FCC Rcd. 11665.

much fluctuation in fees from year to year—because of a combination of annual changes in workload, employee errors in completing time sheets, and various other factors. FCC found that over the 1997 to 1998 period, the rate assessed to all entities in a fee category could increase by more than 25 percent from the prior year—beyond any increase because of increases in the total amount in regulatory fees FCC was required to collect.[20] FCC officials stated that these fluctuations were especially problematic for small service providers that could least absorb unpredictable increases in fees.

According to FCC officials, FCC has continued to rely on the 1998 division of regulatory fees as the basis of its fee division through fiscal year 2011. It has done so in spite of the problems FCC identified with the system and even though this approach put FCC at risk of dividing the regulatory fee burden among entities in different industries based on obsolete data. FCC officials stated that while the statute requires FCC to amend its regulatory fees if FCC determines such amendment is necessary to comply with the FTE-based requirement, among other things, the statute does not prescribe a specific time at which FCC must make such a determination.[21] Furthermore, according to FCC officials, while FCC has maintained information on how its FTEs are distributed among the four core bureaus—which generally track with the four industry sectors—FCC does not have information on how its current FTEs are divided among the fee categories in the current fee schedule.

As a result, for 13 years, FCC has not validated the extent to which its division of fees among industry sectors and fee categories correlates with its current division of FTEs among industry sectors and fee categories. Major changes have occurred in the telecommunications industry since 1998, as described below, making it likely that FCC's fiscal year 1998 FTE analysis no longer reflects FCC's current regulatory priorities. As explained later in the report, FCC's failure to update its FTE analysis is inconsistent with federal guidance on user fees, which, among other

---

[20] *In the Matter of Assessment and Collection of Regulatory Fees for Fiscal Year 1997*, 12 FCC Rcd. 17161, 17165 (1997).

[21] 47 U.S.C. §159(b)(3) states in pertinent part that "The Commission shall, by regulation, amend the Schedule of Regulatory Fees if the Commission determines that the Schedule requires amendment to comply with the requirements of paragraph (1)(A)."

things, emphasizes the importance of regularly updating analyses to ensure that fees are set based on relevant information.

## Changes in the Telecommunications Industry since 1998

The major changes that have occurred in the telecommunications industry over the past 14 years dramatically increase the likelihood that FCC's current division of fees among fee categories has become obsolete. In 2008, FCC stated in a *Further Notice of Proposed Rulemaking* that major industry changes since 1994 included the significant increase of wireless, broadband, and voice over Internet protocol ("VoIP"), and discussed the fact that FCC itself had reorganized several times to reflect industry changes. FCC acknowledged that there could be several areas in which the regulatory fee process could be revised and improved to better reflect the current industry.[22] Two former FCC commissioners told us that the significant increase in broadband and wireless services, the increasing convergence of telecommunications industries, and the transition to digital television are major changes that have occurred since fiscal year 1998 that have affected FCC's workload and priorities.

Changes in FCC's estimates of subscribers, revenues, or other bases used to set the annual regulatory fee rates for different fee categories also indicate major changes in the balance of telecommunications industries from fiscal years 1998 to 2011. According to FCC's estimates (see table 2), measures of some industries grew by over 50 percent—including the wireless telephone industry, for which the number of subscribers grew by over 400 percent—while measures of other industries declined by over 40 percent, including VHF television stations, for which the number of stations declined by 48 percent. In comparison to these dramatic shifts, relatively small changes in the percent of the total regulatory fees expected to be paid by these industries have occurred. For example, while the wireline telephone industry's estimated revenues on which fees are assessed declined by 44 percent from fiscal year 1998 to fiscal year 2011, the percentage of total regulatory fees this industry is expected to pay declined by 4 percentage points, from 48 percent to 44

---

[22]*In the Matter of Assessment and Collection of Regulatory Fees for Fiscal Year 2008*, 24 FCC Rcd 6388, 6401 (2008). FCC has also stated that the statute does not require amendment to the fee schedule to mirror all changes in regulatory costs. See *In the Matter of Assessment and Collection of Regulatory Fees for Fiscal Year 2004*, 19 FCC Rcd., 11665.

percent of total fees. And while the wireless telephone industry's estimated number of subscribers grew 437 percent during this time period, the percentage of the total regulatory fees the cell phone industry is expected to pay grew only 5 percentage points—from 10 to 15 percent of the total regulatory fees. According to FCC officials, there is not always a straightforward relationship between growth in the number of subscribers, revenues, or other basis used to determine the fee rate of a fee category and the amount of work FCC performs related to that fee category, and thus these shifting numbers do not offer a clear guide as to how or even the extent to which the division of FCC's regulatory fees among industry sectors should be realigned. Nevertheless, they reinforce the magnitude of the changes that have occurred, and underscore the likelihood that FCC's division of fees among fee categories may no longer correlate to its current division of FTEs. (See table 2.)

**Table 2: Telecommunications Industry Changes, Fiscal Years 1998 to 2011, as Measured by Basis Used to Set FCC Regulatory Fees**

| Industry and basis used by FCC to set regulatory fees | Fiscal year 1998 estimated number of the basis used by FCC to set regulatory fees | Fiscal year 2011 estimated number of the basis used by FCC to set regulatory fees | Percent change, fiscal year 1998 to 2011 |
|---|---|---|---|
| VHF television stations (number of stations) | 499 | 261 | -48 % |
| Wireline telephone (revenues)[a] | $70,103,000,000 | $39,500,000,000 | -44% |
| Cable (number of subscribers) | 66,000,000 | 63,400,000 | -4% |
| AM/FM radio stations (number of stations) | 8,646 | 10,285 | 19% |
| UHF television stations (number of stations) | 668 | 866 | 30% |
| Geostationary space stations, including operators of direct broadcast satellite television service (number of satellites) | 46 | 87 | 89% |
| Wireless telephone[b] (number of subscribers) | 55,540,000 | 298,000,000 | 437 % |

Source: GAO analysis of FCC data.

[a]Revenue dollars have not been adjusted for inflation.

[b]The fee category that includes wireless telephones is called commercial wireless radio services. It includes specialized mobile radio services, public coast stations, public mobile radio, cellular, 800 MHz air-ground radiotelephone, offshore radio services and broadband personal communications services.

FCC's Office of the Managing Director has published some information that further suggests that FCC is basing its division of regulatory fees among fee categories on data that do not correlate with industry trends and FCC's current workload. In fiscal year 2008, FCC issued a *Further Notice of Proposed Rulemaking (FNPRM)* specifically to consider reforms to its regulatory fee process. In a separate public notice issued after FCC adopted the 2008 *FNPRM*, the Office of the Managing Director provided some updated information on FCC's costs by core bureau.[23] According to FCC officials, the core bureaus correlate to the four industry sectors of wireless telecommunications, wireline telecommunications, media, and international.[24] This information demonstrated substantial misalignment between the division of regulatory fees by industry sector as presented in FCC's fiscal year 2008 *FNPRM* and FCC's costs by bureau in the Wireless, Wireline, and International Bureaus as presented in the public notice, as shown in figure 3—although FCC officials did not include any information at the more granular level of fee category. For example, in fiscal year 2008, the wireless industry paid about 17 percent of the regulatory fees while the Wireless Telecommunications Bureau incurred about 27 percent of FCC's total costs. In contrast, the wireline industry paid about 47 percent of the total fees while the Wireline Competition Bureau incurred about 23 percent of FCC's total costs. FCC did not comprehensively reform its process as a result of this *FNPRM*.[25]

---

[23]Public Notice, 23 FCC Rcd. 14581 (2008).

[24]According to the information provided by the managing director's office, in creating a chart to show fiscal year 2008 total costs by core bureau (see second pie chart of figure 3), FCC staff identified the total estimated costs (both direct and indirect costs) associated with the regulatory activities performed by the four bureaus named in the chart. Estimated indirect costs were comprised of the expenses incurred by the remaining FCC offices and bureaus. Estimated indirect costs were allocated among the four bureaus named in the chart based on their number of FTEs. Estimated costs associated with operating FCC, such as financial operations and human resources, were allocated to each bureau and office based on the number of FTEs in each operating unit, and then allocated to the four bureaus named in the chart based on their number of FTEs.

[25]In the order following this FNPRM, released in May 2009, FCC adopted proposals to eliminate two regulatory fee categories—international fixed public radio and international high frequency broadcast stations—and stated that the outstanding matters stemming from the FNPRM might be decided at a later time in a separate Report and Order. See *In the Matter of Assessment and Collection of Regulatory Fees for Fiscal Year 2009,* 24 FCC Rcd. 5966, footnote 4 (2009).

**Figure 3: FCC's Division of Regulatory Fees versus Costs by Core Bureau, Fiscal Year 2008**

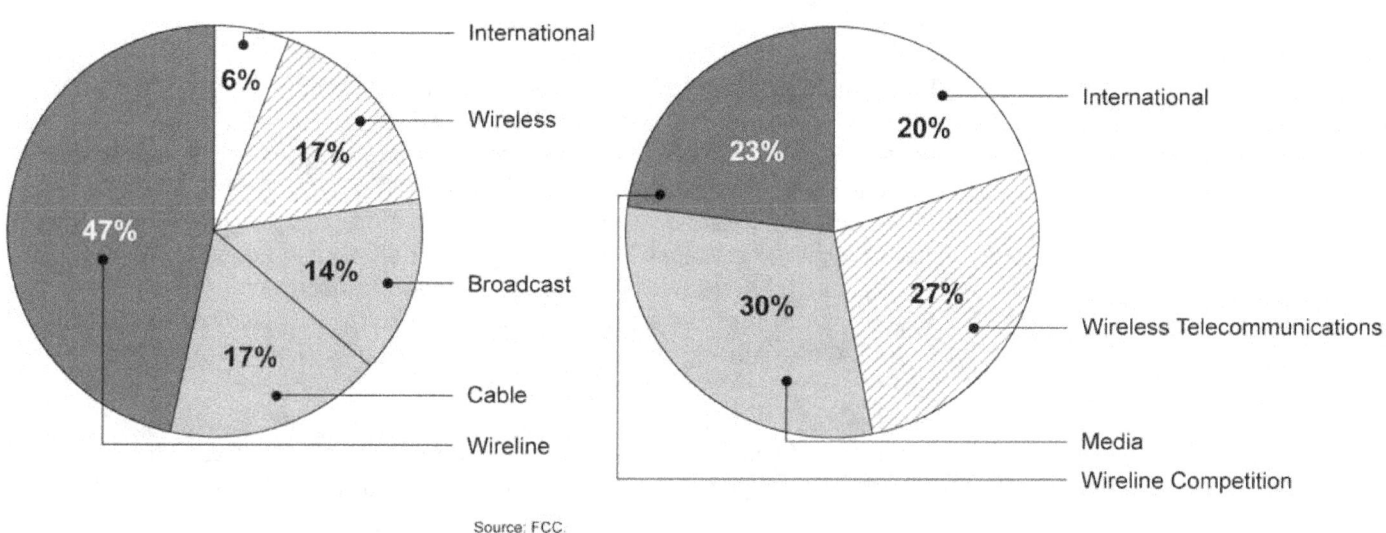

Fiscal year 2008 regulatory fees distributed by
industry sector

Fiscal year 2008 FCC total costs by core bureau

Source: FCC.

## Federal User Fee Guidance

FCC's inaction in updating its FTE analysis is inconsistent with federal guidance on user fees. We recognize that federal guidance on user fees for the most part assumes that the fees are to be set based on a cost-recovery scheme, which differs from the Communications Act's requirement that FCC base its regulatory fees on FTEs, among other things.[26] FTEs—the basic measure of levels of employment used in the

---

[26]User fees are assessed to users for goods or services provided by the federal government that provide special benefits to identifiable recipients above and beyond what is normally available to the public. User fees are normally related to the cost of the goods or services provided. See Office of Management and Budget, *Circular No. A-25 Revised*, (July 8, 1993) and GAO, *A Glossary of Terms Used in the Federal Budget Process*, GAO-05-734SP (Washington, D.C.: September 2005). Regulatory transactions are one type of cost-based user fee. See GAO, *Federal User Fees: A Design Guide*, GAO-08-386SP (Washington, D.C.: May 29, 2008). In addition, the Chief Financial Officers Act of 1990, codified as positive law at 31 U.S.C. ch. 9 requires an agency's CFO to review user fees, among other things, on a biennial basis, and make recommendations on revising those charges to reflect costs incurred. 31 U.S.C. § 902(a)(8). The CFO Act does not apply to FCC, but demonstrates good government practice.

federal budget[27]—are not the same as costs. FTE information is often readily available and can be a useful proxy for cost, but FTE information does not necessarily reflect total cost because, for example, it would neither distinguish between higher and lower cost FTEs, nor would it include other costs, such as contractors, training, equipment, or facilities' costs.[28]

Nevertheless, many of the general principles of federal user fee guidance remain relevant in considering FCC's FTE analysis. First, federal guidance emphasizes the importance of reviewing fees regularly to check the extent to which they are properly aligned. For example, OMB Circular No. A-25, which, among other things, provides guidance to agencies regarding their assessment of user charges under other statutes, directs agencies that have user fees to review the user fees biennially in order to assure, among other things, that existing charges are adjusted to reflect unanticipated changes in costs or market values. The fact that the Communications Act directs FCC to base its fees on FTEs does not negate the applicability of the guidance regarding the regularity with which the basis of the fees (i.e., FTEs) should be reviewed. The reason that regular review is part of the guidance is to assure that fees are adjusted to reflect changes that may have occurred over time in the agency's distribution of work among fee categories—which could be measured by costs or FTEs.

Second, according to federal financial-accounting standards, cost information should be reported in a timely manner and on a regular basis and should be reliable and useful in making decisions. This standard does not require the use of a particular type of costing system or methodology, stating that agency and program management is in the best position to select a type of costing system to meet its needs. However, the standard requires that a methodology, once adopted, be used consistently in order to provide results that can be compared from year to year—with improvements and refinements made as necessary. In FCC's case, given the statutory framework of its regulatory fee program, this principle pertains to FTEs rather than costs. Given the problems FCC encountered with using its cost-accounting system to analyze FTEs by

---

[27]Office of Management and Budget, *Circular No. A-11,* (Aug. 18, 2011).

[28]GAO, *Streamlining Government: Opportunities Exist to Strengthen OMB's Approach to Improving Efficiency,* GAO-10-394 (Washington, D.C.: May 7, 2010).

fee categories in fiscal year 1998, these standards would suggest that FCC could have considered alternate methodologies—or improvements to its cost-accounting system—to address the problems described. However, FCC's decision to freeze its division of regulatory fees by fee category on fiscal year 1998 data that came from the cost-accounting system FCC abandoned, rather than addressing the problems or choosing a different methodology, is inconsistent with the goal of such standards. This decision, over time, has resulted in FCC not having FTE information that is timely, reliable, or comparable from year to year to guide its decisions on how to divide regulatory fees.

## Probable Cross-Subsidization between Industry Sectors

In prior work, we have stated that agencies that do not review and adjust fees regularly run the risk of undercharging or overcharging users, raising equity concerns.[29] Moreover, because FCC is directed in its annual appropriation acts to collect a certain amount of money in regulatory fees each year, if its division of fees among fee categories is misaligned with its FTEs by fee category, then some entities are most likely overpaying, essentially cross-subsidizing entities in other fee categories, which are underpaying.

FCC's regulatory fees are unlikely to ever equal the exact cost of regulating the corresponding fee category for several reasons. First, since FCC is required to collect 100 percent of its appropriation through regulatory fees, including funding for items that are not specifically regulatory activities—such as general overhead—the regulated industries are being assessed to pay for more than the number of FTEs required for their regulation. Second, FCC is directed by statute to base its fee assessment on FTEs, which may not represent actual regulatory costs. According to FCC officials, because it is not possible to precisely assign the costs of regulation on a service-by-service basis, and because the act requires FTE-based assessment and does not require amending the fee schedule to mirror all changes in regulatory costs, some regulated entities pay more than the direct cost of their regulation.

Third, exemptions create cross subsidization, as could some other policy decisions. FCC, as required by statute, has exempted some groups of

---

[29]In past work we defined equity to mean that everyone pays their fair share, acknowledging that the definition of fair share can have multiple facets. See GAO-08-386SP.

entities, such as nonprofits, from paying fees, and has at times exercised its statutory discretion by reducing the fee rates of certain fee categories when it determined that doing so would benefit the public interest. In prior work, we have pointed out that while exemptions can promote one kind of equity by factoring the users' ability to pay into the fee-rate formula, such provisions may also increase cross-subsidies among users.[30] We have stated that in applying exemptions, agencies may purposefully choose to set fees in such a way that cross subsidization occurs in order to promote other policy goals. However, we have also stated that generally, fees should be aligned with the costs of the activities for which the fee is collected, unless there is a policy decision not to align them. Without a current FTE analysis by fee category, it is not possible to determine the extent that cross subsidization is occurring between fee categories, or which fee categories are cross subsidizing other fee categories. However, any cross subsidization that is occurring not because of a decision to promote a policy goal but because the FTE analysis on which FCC bases its fees is obsolete, is not consistent with general user fee principles.

According to officials in many industry associations and companies we spoke with in the wireline, wireless, cable, and international industry sectors, FCC's regulatory fees are typically passed along to the consumer, either in a line item on the bill or bundled into the general cost of service. One potential effect of cross subsidization, therefore, is that, if entities in different fee categories are directly competing for the same customers, cross subsidization could result in competitively disadvantaging entities in one fee category over another. As discussed in the next section, some stakeholders told us that the regulatory fees are small enough that they do not have a significant financial impact on the companies that pay the fees. However, several industry stakeholders in the wireline and cable television industry sectors told us that FCC's current regulatory fee process is competitively disadvantaging certain industries and that FCC's use of multiple bases for setting fee rates makes it more difficult for industry stakeholders to compare the rates assessed to different fee categories—and thus more difficult to determine the extent to which the fees are fair and equitable.

These views were echoed in formal comments to FCC's regulatory fee *FNPRM* in 2008, when FCC last requested comments on substantial

---

[30]GAO-08-386SP.

reform to its regulatory fee process. For example, in response to the 2008 *FNPRM*, the National Cable and Telecommunications Association (NCTA), a trade association for the U.S. cable industry, argued that FCC assesses higher regulatory fees on cable operators than it does on direct broadcast satellite television operators. According to the cable association, the direct broadcast satellite television industry is a direct competitor to cable, and thus its lower regulatory fee burden could give it a competitive advantage. The cable association argued that every type of multichannel video-programming distributor, including cable, telephone, and direct broadcast satellite providers of multichannel video service, should pay the same regulatory fee rate in order to ensure that no entity received the competitive benefit of lower fees based solely on the technology it used. Moreover, the cable association's staff told us that because the cable television industry's fee rate is set on a per-subscriber basis and the direct broadcast satellite television operator industry's fee rate is set on a per-satellite basis, it was not possible to compare the fees as stated in FCC's published information in order to assess their fairness. For the cable association to determine how its members' fees compared to the fees of direct broadcast satellite television operators on a per-subscriber basis, the association had to do its own analysis using company data. In its 2008 comments to the *FNPRM*, the cable association also suggested that all providers of voice service and multichannel video programming distributors—including cable, telephone, and direct broadcast satellite providers—should pay on a per-subscriber basis instead of the three different bases—per revenue dollar, per subscriber, and per satellite—used today.

In another example, the Independent Telephone and Telecommunications Alliance (ITTA), which represents a number of mid-size wireline telephone companies, argued that under FCC's regulatory fee process, wireline companies had higher per-subscriber fees than wireless companies. ITTA argued that this higher per-subscriber rate was not justified because, due to the convergence among technologies since 1994, many of FCC's expenditures related to telecommunications issues now related equally to wireline and wireless providers. According to ITTA, the effect of the different fee rates assessed to wireline and wireless telephone providers was that providers of similar voice services—and their customers—assumed dissimilar responsibility in bearing FCC's regulatory costs.

ITTA called for both wireline and wireless providers' regulatory fees to be assessed on the basis of revenue, instead of the current situation, in which wireline companies pay fees based on revenue while wireless companies pay fees based on subscribership. Interestingly, in fiscal year 1994, FCC assessed the fees of both wireline and wireless telephone entities on the basis of subscribers, as put forth in the fee schedule in the Communications Act.[31] For fiscal year 1995, FCC amended the schedule by, among other things, changing its basis for assessing regulatory fees on the wireline telephone industry from a subscriber to a revenue basis.[32] In making this change, FCC stated in the Report and Order that a revenue-based methodology would equitably distribute the fee requirement in a competitively neutral manner, and that it was FCC's intention to consider changing wireless carriers' fees to a revenue basis in future years. However, FCC has not done so, although wireless providers report the same revenue information to FCC that wireline providers do. In addition, one commenter to a recent *NPRM* suggested that FCC use revenue as the basis for assessing regulatory fees on media fee categories. According to FCC officials, because FCC does not currently require industries in the media fee categories to report any revenue information to FCC, in order for FCC to assess media companies on the basis of revenue, FCC would have to rely on the honor system in determining entities' fee obligations, or establish new reporting requirements, which would be burdensome to FCC and industry.

FCC did not summarize or comment on the proposals submitted by the cable association and ITTA to the fiscal year 2008 *FNPRM*, even though ITTA re-submitted its proposal in response to the fiscal year 2009 *NPRM*. Instead, FCC exercised its administrative discretion to resolve all the outstanding matters stemming from the *FNPRM* at a later time in a separate Report and Order. More than 3 years later, no separate Report and Order has been issued addressing these industry associations' comments. According to NCTA and ITTA officials, the associations stopped submitting formal comments to FCC because FCC's lack of responsiveness discouraged them from doing so—but both associations continue to see the current regulatory fee assessment as not based on any valid FTE analysis and as causing competitive disadvantage to their industry.

---

[31]*See* 47 U.S.C. § 159(g) (Schedule of Regulatory Fees); see also *Implementation of Section 9 of the Communications Act, Assessment and Collection of Regulatory Fees for Fiscal Year 1994*, 9 FCC Rcd. 5333,¶ 9 (1994) recon. denied, 10 FCC Rcd. 12759 ¶12 (1995).

[32]See *In the Matter of Assessment and Collection of Regulatory Fees for Fiscal Year 1995,* 10 FCC Rcd. 13512, 13519 (1995).

## Effect of Fees on Industry and Consumers

Most companies we spoke with stated that FCC's regulatory fees have little to no direct financial impact on the company, given the relatively small size of the fees—for example, wireline telephone companies were to pay $.00375 per assessable revenue dollar in fiscal year 2011, while wireless telephone companies were to pay $0.17 per subscriber. However, officials at the National Association of Broadcasting stated that the payment of regulatory fees is a bigger issue for small stations. These officials stated that because consumers do not pay directly for broadcast radio or television, broadcasting entities cannot pass regulatory fees on to consumers but must incorporate the fee payment into operating costs to be paid with general operating revenue. The National Association of Broadcasters and one broadcast company we spoke with stated that at a time when some broadcasting companies are laying off employees because of financial difficulties, FCC's regulatory fees may equal the cost of one or more employees that the company could not afford to keep because of the regulatory fees. This potential impact on companies underscores the importance that FCC assess regulatory fees on a fair and equitable basis—and that it have updated information on FTEs with which to do so.

The effect of regulatory fees on consumers is difficult to assess, in part because of the relatively low cost of the fees. For example, if a wireless telephone company passed its fiscal year 2011 regulatory fee directly on to consumers, the fee would have increased the bill of each consumer by $0.17 for the year. On the other hand, representatives of a wireline telephone company we spoke with stated that many of their customers are rural, low income, elderly people who are affected by any increase in their phone bill caused by regulatory fees.

## Challenges Related to Regulatory Fee Reform

According to FCC officials, the agency has not revised its assessment of fees among fee categories since fiscal year 1998 in part because it is difficult to propose and implement reforms given its need to collect regulatory fees by the end of each fiscal year. In addition, FCC officials stated that because the agency had received only a limited number of comments to its 2008 *FNPRM*, FCC had decided not to undertake major reform at that time. However, as described above, federal guidance on user fees recommends that agencies review their fees biennially—including the costs that the fees are reimbursing. Moreover, by not periodically analyzing FTEs by fee category and adjusting its division of regulatory fees based on this analysis, FCC may have put itself into a situation where, in order to adjust regulatory fees based on an updated FTE analysis, FCC may have to figure out how to handle large swings in fees for some fee categories. For example, we found that when another agency waited 9 years before performing a review of its cost-based fees, the result was that the average fee increased by 86 percent, causing the new fee schedule to be widely questioned.[33]

Another issue, according to FCC officials, is that assigning regulatory costs among the 86 fee categories has become more challenging, given the increasingly cross-cutting nature of FCC's work. Staff we spoke with in the Wireline, Wireless, and Media Bureaus stated that, generally, their work focuses on the industry sector directly related to their bureau, and that when FCC works on issues that cut across more than one bureau, staff from each relevant bureau will work together. However, staff in the Wireless and Media Bureaus stated that it would be very difficult to track their activities at the level of fee category. Moreover, staff we spoke with in the International and Enforcement Bureaus stated that their work was so cross cutting that they did not think it would make sense to track it according to industry sector—much less according to fee category. This issue is not isolated to FCC's assessment of regulatory fees. In recent work, we found that the increasingly cross-cutting nature of FCC's work has caused FCC to reconsider how to handle some regulatory activities.[34] For example, as companies that once provided a distinct service (such as cable and telephone companies) have shifted to providing bundles of services (voice, video, and data services) over a broadband platform, new debates have arisen at FCC regarding how rules previously intended for a specific industry and service should be applied to companies now providing multiple services. These concerns bring up some additional questions—whether FCC's use of 86 fee categories may also be obsolete in the current regulatory environment, and whether FCC's difficulties in keeping its process current may be in part because its statutory framework is based on a telecommunications environment that no longer exists. However, since FCC has not attempted to track FTEs by fee category since fiscal year 1998, we were not able to determine the extent to which changes since fiscal year 1998—including the increasing amount of cross-cutting work—would affect FCC's ability to distribute its FTEs

---

[33] See GAO, *Federal User Fees: Additional Analyses and Timely Reviews Could Improve Immigration and Naturalization User Fee Design and USCIS Operations*, GAO-09-180 (Washington, D.C.: Jan. 23, 2009).

[34] GAO, *FCC Management: Improvements Needed in Communication, Decision-Making Processes, and Workforce Planning*, GAO-10-79 (Washington, D.C., Dec. 17, 2009).

among the fee categories or what the outcome of such an analysis would be.

In the fiscal year 2012 regulatory fee *NPRM*, released on May 4, 2012, FCC stated that it planned to undertake two separate *NPRMs* to consider reforms to the regulatory fee process. FCC stated that it would issue a Report and Order finalizing its decision on all issues raised in the reform proceedings, including new cost allocations and revised regulatory fees, in sufficient time to allow for their implementation in fiscal year 2013.[35] On July 17, 2012, FCC released an *NPRM* on regulatory fee reform.[36]  As discussed in our agency comments section, this *NPRM* proposes some fundamental changes to FCC's regulatory fee program that relate to many of the concerns raised in this report.

## FCC's Current Regulatory Fee Process Lacks Transparency

FCC has not been transparent in describing its regulatory fee process in its recent annual *NPRMs* and Reports and Orders. This lack of transparency has resulted in uncertainty among some industry associations about FCC's regulatory fee process; some told us that the lack of transparency has made it more difficult for them to comment or provide input on FCC's regulatory fee process. In prior work, we have reported that the regulatory process is used to provide information on fees to Congress and stakeholders and to solicit stakeholder input. Therefore, we have reported that, when an agency has authority to adjust a fee through the regulatory process, as a first step towards improved transparency, it should make available to the public substantive information about recent and projected program costs and fee collections through its notices in the *Federal Register*. Relevant information includes the agency's new fee rates, descriptions of the costs of the program, projected program costs and fee collections, and the assumptions the agency used to make those projections.[37]

FCC's recent annual Reports and Orders on regulatory fees include FCC's fee rates, along with the total FCC is required to collect as directed

---

[35]*In the Matter of Assessment and Collection of Regulatory Fees for Fiscal Year 2012,* FCC 12-48 (May 4, 2012).

[36] In *the Matter of Procedures for Assessment and Collection of Regulatory Fees*, FCC 12-77, July 17, 2012.

[37]GAO-08-386SP, p. 35.

in its appropriations act and how much it expects to collect from each fee category. However, since FCC has not performed any current FTE analysis, there is no discussion of FCC's current FTEs or costs related to each fee category. Moreover, FCC does not clearly explain in any of the Reports and Orders after fiscal year 2002 that the division of regulatory fees among fee categories is based on a fiscal year 1998 FTE analysis that was never updated. This lack of information in FCC's regulatory-fee-related *NPRMs* and Reports and Orders has limited the ability of industry stakeholders to understand exactly how FCC has been determining its assessment of regulatory fees in recent years, and may have limited stakeholders' ability to effectively provide input to this process.

Another area where FCC has not been transparent is in describing the effects of its adjustments on other fee payors. Each year, FCC's regulatory-fee-related *NPRMs* and Reports and Orders include any proposed or actual adjustments and tables detailing the resulting regulatory fees for all payors. However, those tables have not explicitly shown how adjustments to the rates of certain fee categories have affected the rates of the other fee categories, or the total FCC must attempt to collect from other fee categories. Consequently, it is difficult to use FCC's information to determine how FCC got from the previous year's regulatory fee rates to the current year's regulatory fee rates.

For example, in the fiscal year 2010 Report and Order, FCC stated that because the revenue base upon which the wireline telephone industry's fee rate is calculated had been decreasing for several years, FCC had determined it would best serve the public interest to set the wireline telephone industry's fiscal year 2010 fee rate at $0.00349 per revenue dollar. In a footnote, FCC elaborated that because the wireline telephone industry's revenue data was lower than expected, if FCC had not decided to set the wireline telephone rate at $0.00349 per revenue dollar, the rate would have increased to $0.00364 per revenue dollar. However, FCC did not explain what this change in rates translated to in terms of the amount of revenue it expected to collect in fees from the wireline telephone industry. Moreover, while FCC stated in the Report and Order that reducing the fees paid by the wireline telephone industry would increase the fees paid by licensees in other service categories, and the resulting regulatory fees are detailed in FCC's Report and Order, FCC did not specifically show the fee increase for each regulatory fee category caused solely by this policy decision. In November 2011, FCC officials told us that this policy decision had resulted in reducing the total expected fees to be collected from the wireline telephone industry by approximately $12 million, and that FCC instead attempted to collect this $12 million by raising the rates of all the other fee categories based on the existing division of fees among fee categories. This $12 million is reflected in the regulatory fee tables set forth in FCC's Order. However, the limited information on how various adjustments affect each fee category reduces the ease with which industry stakeholders or other interested parties can understand the effects of FCC's current process—including the policy decisions FCC has made without any updated FTE analysis.

# FCC Has Collected $66 Million in Excess Fees That Is Unavailable without Further Congressional Action

## FCC's Regulatory Fee Collections

On average, FCC collected 2 percent more each year in regulatory fees than it was required to collect in its annual appropriations acts over the past 10 fiscal years.[38] FCC under collected regulatory fees in 1 year—2003—and over collected regulatory fees in 9 years. For example, it overcollected regulatory fees by 5 percent—$13 million—in fiscal year 2005. (See table 3.)

---

[38]In fiscal year 2002, FCC was directed to collect 89 percent of its appropriation in regulatory fees. In fiscal year 2003, FCC was directed to collect 99 percent of its appropriation. For fiscal years 2004 to 2008, FCC was directed to collect all but $1 million of its appropriation in regulatory fees, and since fiscal year 2009, FCC has been directed to collect 100 percent of its appropriation in regulatory fees.

**Table 3: FCC's Regulatory Fee Collections, Fiscal Years 2002 to 2011**

(In millions)

| Fiscal Year | Amount of regulatory fees FCC was required to collect | Amount of regulatory fees FCC collected | Percentage difference between fees required to collect and fees collected |
|---|---|---|---|
| 2002 | $219 | $220 | 1% |
| 2003 | $269 | $266 | -1% |
| 2004 | $273 | $285 | 5% |
| 2005 | $280 | $293 | 5% |
| 2006 | $299 | $308 | 3% |
| 2007 | $290 | $297 | 2% |
| 2008 | $312 | $325 | 4% |
| 2009 | $342 | $342[a] | 0% |
| 2010 | $336 | $342 | 2% |
| 2011 | $336 | $342 | 2% |

Source: GAO analysis of FCC data.

[a]FCC collected $81,000 more in regulatory fees than it was directed to collect in fiscal year 2009.

According to FCC officials, FCC attempts to meet its regulatory fee target each year but is unable to ensure it will collect exactly the amount required by Congress because there are multiple variables that can affect the final amount collected. Key variables that can cause FCC to collect more or less than it expected are late payments, FCC's use of preliminary data in setting fee rates, refunds, and bankruptcies. Regarding late payments, FCC counts all regulatory fee payments that arrive in a fiscal year as part of that year's regulatory fee collections, even if the imposed assessment was incurred in a prior year. FCC officials stated that each year some entities do not pay the fees owed that year, while some entities pay fees owed from prior years. According to FCC officials, because in any given year, FCC does not know exactly how much of the year's owed fees are not going to be paid in the year they are due, or how much in late payments will come in from prior years, late payments can affect the total amount of regulatory fees collected for the year. We found that the percentage of FCC's total annual regulatory fee collections that was made up of late payments varied from 1 to 3 percent for fiscal years 2005 to 2011.

FCC's use of preliminary data to set fees also can cause FCC to collect more or less than it expected and can at times lead to FCC's having to refund companies some of their prior year's fees, which can also affect the total collected. In order to charge fees based on current year data and to publish the final fee rates in the Report and Order in time for entities to pay by the end of the fiscal year, FCC must set the fee rate for some large fee categories—including wireline telephones, wireless telephones, and cable, among others—based on preliminary industry information. For example, until fiscal year 2011, FCC relied on preliminary estimates provided to FCC by wireline telephone entities to estimate the total amount of revenue dollars in the wireline telephone industry.[39] In combination with FCC projections based on past years' collections and economic conditions, FCC set the wireline telephone fee rate based on this preliminary industry data. Wireline telephone entities determine the amount of fees they owe by multiplying the fee rate as published in FCC's annual Report and Order by their final revenue dollars, as reported by the entities typically after FCC had already set the rate for the fiscal year. If, in aggregate, the total final amount of revenue dollars in the industry was significantly higher or lower than the estimate FCC used to set the fee rate, FCC would collect more or less than it expected.

In fiscal year 2011, FCC automated the input of annual revenue data provided by wireline providers to FCC so FCC would have actual instead of estimated revenue information to use in setting regulatory fees for wireline telephone companies. According to FCC officials, this change should improve FCC's ability to predict how much total revenue wireline telephone entities will pay fees on, and therefore improve the accuracy of the rate it sets for the wireline telephone fee category in terms of meeting its target collection amount from that fee category. However, even so, wireline telephone entities can revise their final revenue numbers for an entire year after the revenue information has been submitted. According to FCC officials, if some wireline telephone entities pay their regulatory fees based on the revenue information submitted in one fiscal year, but then revise their revenue numbers downward after the end of the fiscal year, the filer may be entitled to a refund in the following year, which also can affect FCC's ability to collect exactly the targeted amount in the next fiscal year. According to FCC officials, refunds can be sought on other

---

[39]Only certain wireline telephone companies' revenues are used in setting their fee. In this paragraph, we are referring to those revenues.

grounds, too, and such filings cannot be predicted by FCC. In addition, according to FCC officials, FCC is an unsecured creditor when it comes to a licensee filing for bankruptcy and FCC often does not receive unpaid assessments from the bankruptcy court. Therefore, bankruptcies can also affect FCC's ability to collect its target amount.

## Excess Regulatory Fees

Any regulatory fees collected above what FCC was directed to collect in its annual appropriations are considered excess fees. As explained earlier, since 2008, FCC's annual appropriations have prohibited the use of any excess fees from the current year or previous years without an appropriation by Congress. Prior to fiscal year 2008, FCC's annual appropriations stated that any excess regulatory fees remained available until expended. According to FCC officials, FCC obligated excess regulatory fees in fiscal years 1996 to 1998 to fund programs to help FCC with changes related to the year 2000 technology transition (sometimes referred to as Y2K), and it obligated excess regulatory fees from 2001 to 2003[40] in order to meet critical physical security needs in fiscal year 2004.[41] According to FCC officials, FCC has deposited all excess fee collections into a separate account with the Department of Treasury.[42] As of fiscal year 2011, the account held approximately $66 million, which represents about 2 percent of the $2.9 billion FCC was required to collect in regulatory fees from fiscal year 2002 to 2010.[43] FCC has collected on average $6.7 million in excess fees annually from fiscal year 2006 to 2011, and so the account has steadily increased. FCC's tendency to over collect rather than under collect regulatory fees over the past 10 years

[40]Disbursements from FCC's excess regulatory fee account were made through fiscal year 2006.

[41]FCC was unable to identify the purposes for which it obligated excess regulatory fee collection prior to fiscal year 1999 because FCC does not retain records prior to fiscal year 2000.

[42]According to FCC officials, for fiscal year 2003, the 1 year out of the past 10 that FCC under collected its regulatory fees (by $5 million, or about 2 percent), FCC reimbursed the Department of Treasury the amount that it collected in regulatory fees and notified the Department of Treasury and Congress. According to FCC officials, no further action was taken. As a result, FCC did not fully offset its appropriation for fiscal year 2003.

[43]At the end of fiscal year 2011, FCC's excess collections account had a balance of $66 million dollars, of which $5.3 million dollars had been deposited prior to fiscal year 2002. Because of limitations with FCC's data, GAO was unable to determine a year-by-year breakdown of excess collections for fiscal years prior to 2002.

also suggests that as long as Congress does not provide for their disposition, total excess funds will continue to increase. Congress has not provided for the disposition of the funds.

According to FCC officials, FCC has reported to Congress and the Department of Treasury on its excess regulatory fees. However, FCC has not been fully transparent with regard to informing industry stakeholders or others about these excess fees. FCC officials stated that FCC has kept Congress informed of the excess fees during periodic briefings with appropriators, and FCC provides an annual report to Treasury that identifies the total amount of regulatory fees it has collected for the past year, including the extent to which its collections vary from the amount FCC is required to collect. FCC also published the amount of excess fees collected in its fiscal year 2011 *Annual Financial Report* and its fiscal year 2013 budget estimate to Congress. However, FCC has not published the amount of excess fees collected in its *NPRMs* or Reports and Orders. In prior work, we have reported that the regulatory process is used to provide information on fees to stakeholders and to solicit stakeholder input.[44] Therefore, when an agency has authority to adjust a fee through the regulatory process, it should make substantive information about recent and projected fee collections, among other things, available to the public through notices in the *Federal Register*. FCC has included projected fee collections for the current fiscal year in its *NPRMs* and Reports and Orders, but it has not disclosed the actual amount collected the prior year or disclosed any information on the total in excess fees collected in previous years. As a result, some industry associations we spoke with were aware that FCC had collected excess regulatory fees, but most did not know that the amount of FCC's excess collections had grown to about $66 million.

---

[44]GAO-08-386SP.

## Alternative Approaches Could Be Instructive as FCC Considers Reforms to Its Regulatory Fee Process

We identified alternative approaches that could be instructive as FCC considers reforms to its regulatory fee process. These alternative approaches include (1) ensuring that the division of fees among fee categories is aligned with a reasonably current measure of the division of regulatory activities among fee categories, and (2) taking specific steps to promote transparency in the regulatory fee process. In addition, we identified how these agencies are applying any excess fees.

We identified these alternative approaches through examining the regulatory fee processes of five other regulatory fee-funded agencies in the U.S. and Canada: the Nuclear Regulatory Commission (NRC), Federal Energy Regulatory Commission (FERC), Farm Credit Administration (FCA), Canadian Radio-television and Telecommunications Commission (CRTC), and the Canadian Nuclear Safety Commission (CNSC). Because these agencies perform regulatory functions and recover many, if not all, of their costs through annual fees paid by regulated entities, we believe their processes may be instructive to FCC and Congress in considering reforms to FCC's current regulatory fee process. In addition, while four of the agencies regulate different industries, CRTC regulates some of the same industries as FCC, including, according to CRTC officials, the telecommunications industry—which encompasses wireline and wireless telephone providers—and the broadcast industry—which encompasses radio, television, and cable distribution operators. Each of the five agencies, like FCC, has different, specific statutory authority authorizing its collection of annual regulatory fees to help fund the agency or to reimburse the Department of Treasury for its annual appropriation.[45] FERC, for example, which has regulatory authority over the hydropower, oil pipeline, natural gas, and electric industries, derives its fee-collecting authorities from the Federal Power Act for the hydropower industry and the Omnibus Budget Reconciliation Act of 1986 for the oil, natural gas and electricity industries.[46] Nevertheless, we believe approaches used by these agencies may be instructive for FCC as it considers reforms to its regulatory fee process. For more information on the criteria used to select these agencies, see appendix I.

---

[45]Some of the agencies also collect hourly fees for specific regulatory work done in addition to the annual regulatory fees which are the focus of this report.

[46]See Act of June 10, 1920, ch. 285, 41 Stat. 1063 (codified at 16 U.S.C. § 803, § 823a) and Pub. L. No. 99-509, § 3401, 100 Stat. 1874 (1986) (codified at 42 U.S.C. § 7178).

## Ensuring Data Used to Align Fees with Regulatory Activities Is Reasonably Current

As we described previously, FCC has acknowledged the need to revisit its division of fees among fee categories to reflect regulatory and staffing changes that have occurred since 1998. However, it has not yet done so. We found that NRC, CRTC, and FERC divide fees among fee categories based on current or recent data by industry sector. The other two agencies we met with either have only one fee category (FCA) or do not collect most fees through a rate assessed to a category of fee payors (CNSC).

According to officials at NRC, CRTC, and FERC, each agency aligns its assessment of annual fees by industry sector with an annually or biennially updated analysis of costs by industry sector. Officials at NRC specifically stated that keeping the agency's fees aligned with annually or biennially updated costs was essential to ensuring that the fees were fair and equitable. If one industry sector gets more in services or regulatory activities from NRC in one year compared to the previous year, then that sector will pay a higher proportion of the total regulatory fees. NRC officials stated that they consider it part of NRC's mission as a regulatory agency to ensure that the link between costs and fees is apparent, and officials at both NRC and CRTC told us that it is important that the regulated industries understand the rationale for the assessed fees. As stated previously, the Communications Act identifies FTEs as FCC's basis for deriving regulatory fees. Nevertheless, the methods these three agencies use to keep their alignment of costs and fees updated may be instructive to FCC.

According to NRC officials, NRC updates its cost analysis for its larger fee categories annually and its smaller fee categories biennially. The officials added that NRC's regulatory fees are based on the proportional cost of direct and indirect services provided to an industry sector, as determined by NRC's program offices, compared to the total fee-funded budget—and there is a direct link between the resources planned in the budget and the distribution of regulatory fees. For example, NRC officials stated that because the nuclear reactor category accounted for approximately 88 percent of the NRC fee-funded budget in fiscal year 2010, the nuclear reactor category was responsible for approximately 88 percent of the fees collected for fiscal year 2010. NRC officials told us that because they analyze costs for NRC's larger fee categories annually and revise their division of fees accordingly by industry sector, at times an industry sector's proportion of fees has risen or fallen compared to the previous year. However, NRC officials stated that the industries they regulate are generally aware of what work NRC plans to do related to each industry sector—in part because NRC informs industry of its plans during its budget process.

CRTC also links the division of its fees by fee category to its costs for regulating each fee category, and CRTC updates its cost analysis and its fee assessment annually. One element of CRTC's process that may be instructive to FCC in considering reforms is that while according to CRTC officials, CRTC regulates many of the same converging industries in Canada that FCC regulates in the United States, CRTC has only two fee categories for assessing regulatory fees: telecommunications and broadcast. Like FCC, CRTC regulates wireline telephone, wireless telephone, direct broadcast satellite and cable television operators, broadcast television, and radio.[47] However, CRTC has one broadcast fee category that includes radio stations, television stations, and cable and direct broadcast satellite television operators. All pay the same rate on the same basis—the licensee's fee revenues for the most recently completed year. In contrast, FCC has 62 fee categories for the same broadcasting services, and different bases for different fee categories, including, among others, a flat fee for each fee category of broadcast television and radio station, a per-subscriber fee rate for cable television, and a per-satellite fee rate for direct broadcasting satellite television operators.

In another example, CRTC's telecommunications fee category encompasses wireless telephone services and wireline telephone services. The rate for the telecommunications fee category is set on the same basis used to set the rate for the broadcast industry—the licensee's fee revenues for the most recently completed year. In contrast, FCC has separate fee categories for wireless telephone services and wireline telephone services—and the two fee categories pay different rates set on different bases, with the wireless telephone rate set on a per-subscriber basis and the wireline telephone rate set on a per-revenue-dollar basis.

CRTC officials told us that having two fee categories—both with fee rates determined on the basis of revenue—makes it relatively easy for CRTC to align costs to a fee category, even given the increasing convergence of industry and the cross-cutting nature of CRTC's work. CRTC officials told

---

[47]Some of the industry sectors FCC regulates are regulated in Canada by another Canadian agency, Industry Canada, including the submarine cable industry. In addition, unlike FCC, CRTC does not manage spectrum, which is managed by Industry Canada.

us they track CRTC's direct costs according to these fee categories in CRTC's activity-based cost system annually. Because most mission-related staff are assigned to work centers aligned with either the broadcasting or the telecommunications industries, CRTC officials said it is administratively easy to track costs according to these fee categories. For staff working on cross-cutting issues related to both categories, management estimates how much time each staff has spent on each of the two fee categories.[48] CRTC then divides the total amount in fees it must collect between the two fee categories based on its costs associated with each fee category. Indirect costs for internal services provided to the entire agency—such as, among other things, human resources, legal services, and accounting—are divided among the two fee categories consistent with the distribution of direct costs.

FERC also tracks its costs by industry sector and fee category annually and then assesses fees in alignment with its costs. FERC officials told us that FERC's time and attendance system tracks the time staff spends directly on each fee category through activity codes aligned with particular fee categories. This assessment of time spent on each industry forms the basis of the assessment of fees. Similar to CRTC, indirect costs are assessed among the fee categories based on the assessment of direct costs incurred by industry sector.

## Making the Assessment Process Transparent

NRC takes specific steps that facilitate industry and public understanding of how the agency distributes and assesses regulatory fees that go beyond FCC's provision of information on this topic. NRC officials stated that NRC's chief financial officer has consistently emphasized the importance of transparency in setting fees. According to NRC officials, transparency is important because the fees impact NRC's stakeholders, and therefore stakeholders should be able to understand how the fees are derived. While both FCC and NRC publish *NPRMs* and Final Orders regarding each year's fees, NRC also publishes the workpapers it has used to determine the fees and rates in its *NPRMs* and Final Orders to

---

[48]Before CRTC began estimating the time staff spent on cross-cutting issues, officials told us they had used an activity-based costing system to account for all staff time spent on each category. CRTC leadership later asked the managers in each category to estimate the distribution of staff time. According to officials we met with, the estimates were close enough to the results of the activity-based costing system that CRTC determined it wasn't cost-effective to continue using its activity-based costing system for this purpose.

further promote transparency. These workpapers contain detailed cost data that form NRC's basis for setting its fees for each industry sector. NRC's website has a link to an electronic docket that contains its regulatory-fee-related *NPRM*, Final Order, and workpapers, such that one can see how NRC went from its detailed cost data to its final fee-setting rule. As described previously, in recent years, FCC has not included this level of detail in its *NPRMs* and Reports and Orders related to its regulatory fees. Moreover, in addition to providing these supporting workpapers on its website, NRC staff told us they also meet with industry stakeholders periodically to help ensure the stakeholders understand the assessment process and how the fee rates are determined.

## Handling of Excess Fees

As mentioned earlier, FCC may not obligate any excess fees it receives without an appropriation from Congress. In contrast, officials at all five agencies we met with told us their agency has a form of annual adjustment or "true-up" mechanism such that any excess fees collected are either applied as an adjustment to the next year's fees or are refunded. Four of the five agencies apply any excess fees collected toward the next year's fee assessment, while one agency issues a refund. For example, according to NRC's fiscal year 2011 *Annual Financial Report*, NRC applies collections that exceed its budget authority to offset subsequent years' appropriations. According to FERC officials, at year-end, FERC calculates a required subsequent year adjustment based on the difference between the amounts assessed and actual costs. CRTC officials told us that they make an adjustment to the subsequent year's assessments based on the difference between the fees collected—based on estimated costs—and annual expenditures. FCA officials stated that FCA also makes adjustments for overpayments in the current year to fees owed the following year. Lastly, CNSC officials told us they refund fees collected in excess of actual costs. As a result of these procedures, the fees paid to these five agencies are ultimately used to fund the regulatory agency or are refunded.

## Conclusions

The Communications Act states that FCC is to derive regulatory fees from the number of FTEs in certain bureaus performing regulatory activities, but the act does not specifically state how frequently FCC must reexamine its FTEs to assure its regulatory fees are aligned with FCC's current work priorities. FCC has relied on this lack of clarity to justify continuing to use 1998 data as the basis for its assessment of regulatory fees—in spite of the vast changes to the telecommunications industry that have occurred, including significant convergence of technologies and changes in the nature of the industries that FCC regulates. Federal user fee guidance, accounting standards, and the practices of other agencies we met with all stress the importance of using timely, regularly updated data to guide decisions, with federal user fee guidance directing agencies to review user fees biennially to assure that charges are adjusted to reflect changes that have occurred. In addition, although FCC has made incremental changes to the fee schedule first established in the Communications Act and implemented by FCC in fiscal year 1994, FCC has not considered more holistic changes to the way regulatory fees are assessed. In part, FCC's difficulties in keeping its process current may be because its statutory framework is based on a telecommunications environment that no longer exists. The large number of fee categories—86 in fiscal year 2011—may have contributed to FCC's difficulties in keeping the division of fees aligned with the current regulatory activities on which it spends its time. Furthermore, FCC's lack of transparency in disclosing its methodology for dividing regulatory fees among fee categories and the different methodologies FCC uses to calculate fee rates for different industries have made it difficult for stakeholders to understand and comment on FCC's decisions related to its regulatory fee process.

On July 17, 2012, FCC released an *NPRM* on regulatory fee reform, which, as described in our agency comments section, contains proposals that respond to many of the concerns raised in this report. The processes of other regulatory fee-funded agencies, both in the United States and internationally, may be instructive for FCC as it considers such issues as re-aligning its division of regulatory fees and increasing the transparency of the process. We acknowledge the inherent difficulties in reforming the process. Because of the zero-sum nature of FCC's regulatory fees, any significant changes to FCC's assessment of regulatory fees among industry sectors and fee categories would most likely result in fee increases for some sectors and fee decreases for other sectors. Not only is this likely to be controversial to some industry stakeholders, but this change—and any analysis required to better align regulatory fees to FCC's division of FTEs by fee category—is likely to be time consuming and require some FCC resources, if done comprehensively. Some potential changes, such as changes to the bases on which FCC assesses regulatory fees—could add new administrative burdens on FCC or industry stakeholders. The likely effects of changes to its current fee assessment will need to be carefully analyzed by FCC. In releasing the regulatory fee reform *NPRM*, FCC has taken an important first step in this challenging reform effort, but significant analysis and decisions remain to be made by FCC.

Lastly, over time, FCC has collected approximately 2 percent more on average than is required in its annual appropriations acts. Because recent annual appropriations do not permit FCC to use any of these excess fees without congressional action, they currently have grown to $66 million and, absent any change in FCC's statutory authority and method of collecting fees, are likely to continue to increase. The decision of how to dispose of these excess regulatory fees as well as how to handle any future excess collections is a policy choice for Congress to make.

## Matter for Congressional Consideration

Congress should consider whether FCC's excess fees (approximately $66 million through fiscal year 2011) should be appropriated for FCC's use, or, if not, what the disposition of these funds should be, and whether to change FCC's annual appropriations language to permit reconciliation of excess collections or to govern FCC's handling of any future excess collections.

## Recommendations for Executive Action

We recommend that the Chairman of the FCC, as part of FCC's effort to reform its regulatory fee process, take the following three actions:

- Determine whether and how the current fee schedule should be revised—including an overall analysis of the appropriate number of categories and bases for calculating rates—to reflect the current telecommunications industry and FCC's regulatory activities, and in consideration of the processes of other regulatory fee-funded agencies that may be instructive, including, if appropriate, proposing to Congress any needed changes to its current statutory authority.

- Perform an updated FCC FTE analysis by fee category and establish a process to assure that the FTE analysis be performed at least biennially, consistent with federal guidance on user fees.

- Increase the transparency of FCC's regulatory fee process by describing in each future year's *NPRM* and subsequent report, in sufficient detail for stakeholders to understand, the methodology and analysis used to divide fees among fee categories, including the year any FTE data used was collected, any additional information needed to explain the effect of other adjustments, and the amount of excess fees collected.

## Agency Comments

FCC provided written comments on a draft of this report by letter dated July 17, 2012. These comments are summarized below and are reprinted in appendix II. FCC agreed with our recommendations and stated that an *NPRM* on regulatory fee reform, released on July 17, 2012, addressed them. FCC stated that the *NPRM* sets forth three goals to guide FCC in its reform initiative: fairness, administrability, and sustainability. FCC stated that to achieve these goals, the Commission has proposed a series of fundamental changes to its regulatory fee program that include, but are not limited to, proposals contained in our recommendations. For example, FCC stated that, consistent with our recommendations, the *NPRM* seeks comment on (1) using updated fiscal year 2012 FTE data to calculate regulatory fees, (2) whether reducing the number of regulatory fee categories would be advisable, and (3) whether the different bases on which regulatory fees are currently calculated should be reduced or made uniform among all services. FCC stated that, consistent with our recommendation to consider the processes of other regulatory fee-funded agencies, it would place a copy of our final report in the record of the rulemaking so that interested parties could comment on our recommendations and analyses. Regarding our recommendation that FCC review its division of FTEs at least biennially, FCC stated that its *NPRM* seeks comment on the frequency with which FCC should revisit its division of FTEs, such as annually. Furthermore, FCC stated that it would implement our recommendation to increase the transparency of its rulemaking process in its next annual regulatory fee proceeding, for fiscal year 2013. Finally, regarding our matter for congressional consideration related to excess fees, FCC stated that should Congress decide to examine these or any other issues regarding regulatory fees, FCC would provide any information Congress may request. We recognize that the proposals contained in FCC's *NPRM* are responsive to our recommendations. In light of FCC's lack of action after its 2008 *FNPRM* on regulatory fee reform, it remains critical that FCC continue to move forward on analyzing its proposals and determining how best to update its regulatory fee process.

As agreed with your offices, unless you publicly announce the contents of this report earlier, we plan no further distribution until 30 days from the date of this report. At that time, we will send copies to the Chairman of FCC and other interested parties. In addition, the report will be available at no charge on the GAO website at http://www.gao.gov.

If you or your staffs have any questions about this report, please contact me at (202) 512-2834 or goldsteinm@gao.gov. Contact points for our Offices of Congressional Relations and Public Affairs may be found on the last page of this report. GAO staff who made major contributions to this report are listed in appendix III.

Mark L. Goldstein
Director
Physical Infrastructure Issues

# Appendix I: Objectives, Scope and Methodology

In response to your request to review FCC's regulatory fee process, we examined (1) FCC's process for assessing regulatory fees among industry sectors and the results of this process, (2) FCC's regulatory fee collections over the past 10 years compared to the amount it was directed to collect by Congress, and (3) alternative approaches to assessing and collecting regulatory fees that could be instructive for FCC as it considers reforms to its process.

In examining FCC's regulatory fee process, we reviewed relevant federal statutes, federal appropriations acts, congressional reports and hearing transcripts, FCC documents, and GAO reports. We spoke to stakeholders, including officials at FCC, industry trade associations, and fee-paying companies. Specifically, among others, we reviewed the following documents:

- Statute establishing FCC's regulatory fee-collecting authority (Section 9 of the Communications Act of 1934)

- FCC's appropriations acts, fiscal years 1994 to 2011

- Conference Report to Accompany the Federal Communications Commission Authorization Act of 1991, Sept. 17, 1991

- Hearing transcript, House Energy and Commerce Subcommittee on Communications and Technology Hearing on President Obama's Fiscal 2013 Budget Proposal for the Federal Communications Commission, February 16, 2012

- FCC Notices of Proposed Rulemakings, Further Notice of Proposed Rulemaking, and Reports and Orders related to FCC's collection of regulatory fees, fiscal years 1994 through 2012

- FCC budget justifications, fiscal years 2005 to 2013

- FCC internal documentation of its regulatory fee methodology

- FCC internal documentation related to its core financial system, Genesis

- FCC strategic plans, 2009 to 2014 and 2012 to 2016

- FCC annual financial reports, fiscal years 2010 and 2011

- Prior GAO work on FCC, regulatory agencies, and user fees

- Federal guidance on user fees and cost accounting, including the Office of Management and Budget's Circular No. A-25 and the *Statement of Federal Financial Accounting Standards 4.*

We also spoke with stakeholders from the following entities:

- FCC—Office of the Managing Director, Enforcement Bureau, International Bureau, Media Bureau, Wireless Telecommunications Bureau, Wireline Competition Bureau

- Two former FCC commissioners

- Industry associations—American Association of Paging Carriers, CTIA-The Wireless Association, Independent Telephone & Telecommunications Alliance, National Association of Broadcasters, National Cable and Telecommunications Association, US Telecom

- Fee-paying Companies—Commonwealth Broadcasting, Critical Alert Systems, DIRECTV, Gannett Company Inc./Multimedia Holdings Corp., Intelsat, KRIS-TV, Level 3 Communications, Mainline Broadcasting, Midcontinent Media, People's Telco, Quincy Newspapers (regarding its TV and radio interests), Southern Utah Telephone Company, Windstream Communications, and WUBU-FM

To select the fee-paying companies (listed above) to interview about their perspectives on FCC's regulatory fee process, we began with a list of companies provided by FCC. Our criteria for selecting companies from the FCC list were as follows:

- companies from each industry sector (wireless, wireline, broadcasting, cable, international);

- companies from a variety of fee codes within the industry sectors; and

- an emphasis on small companies, as they may be less well represented in associations, less likely to submit public comments to regulatory fee rulemakings, and regulatory fees may impact them more.

Within each industry sector and fee category, we selected companies using these criteria and a few additional constraints. For example, if an

FM radio station in a small market appeared to be owned by a company
that also owned a station in a large market, then we treated it as large.
Also, in most cases, companies were selected based on the fee
categories in which they conducted their primary business, not on
secondary business they might also have conducted.

To understand FCC's regulatory fee collections over the past 10 years
compared to the amount it was directed to collect by Congress, we (1)
met with officials to discuss FCC fee collection process and timeline and
(2) analyzed FCC regulatory fee collection data from FCC's internal
financial system, Genesis, by FCC's "payment type code" from fiscal year
2002 to fiscal year 2011. We assessed the reliability of the data through
reviewing documentation on Genesis, and through interviews
supplemented with questionnaires to knowledgeable agency officials on
Genesis and related internal controls. We determined that the data were
sufficiently reliable for determining FCC's total regulatory fee collections,
including by industry sector, for fiscal years 2002 through 2011, and for
determining the amount of late payments in each of those years. We
compared this fee collection data with the amount Congress appropriated
to FCC for each respective year. FCC's payment type codes are codes
FCC assigns to identify the fee category for which a regulatory fee
payment is associated with. FCC officials also provided us with a cross-
reference that associated payment type codes with the main industry
sectors used in our review (i.e., Broadcast, Cable, Wireline, Wireless, and
International.) Subsequently, we analyzed the fee payment data by
industry sector to understand the extent, if any, to which excess fees
collected were associated with a particular industry sector and to analyze
the influence of late payments on the total amount collected. We also
spoke with a budgeting and forecasting expert, who provided background
information and context related to FCC's use of estimates and forecasts
in setting regulatory fees.

To identify alternative approaches to FCC's regulatory fee process that
could be instructive as FCC considers reforms to its current process, we
reviewed the regulatory fee processes of several foreign and domestic
federal agencies. In selecting comparative agencies, we narrowed our
scope to those agencies that were similar enough to FCC in mission and
fee process such that possibly instructive alternatives could be identified.
FCC is an independent agency that regulates interstate and international
communications by radio, television, wire, satellite and cable, and that
assesses annual regulatory fees to offset its entire annual appropriation
from Congress. We therefore selected independent regulatory
commissions that recover the majority or all of their costs through annual

fees assessed on regulated entities, including, in the U.S., the (1) Nuclear
Regulatory Commission, (2) Federal Energy Regulatory Commission, and
(3) The Farm Credit Administration. In order to include an agency that
regulates industries that are similar to those regulated by FCC, we also
included (4) the Canadian Radio-television and Telecommunications
Commission (CRTC). Lastly, after receiving a recommendation from an
official at CRTC, we included (5) the Canadian Nuclear Safety
Commission, the Nuclear Regulatory Commission's Canadian
counterpart.

We conducted this performance audit from May 2011 to August 2012 in
accordance with generally accepted government auditing standards.
Those standards require that we plan and perform the audit to obtain
sufficient, appropriate evidence to provide a reasonable basis for our
findings and conclusions based on our audit objectives. We believe that
the evidence obtained provides a reasonable basis for our findings and
conclusions based on our audit objectives.

# Appendix II: Comments from the Federal Communications Commission

Federal Communications Commission
Washington, D.C. 20554

July 17, 2012

Mark L. Goldstein
Director, Physical Infrastructure Issues
U.S. Government Accountability Office
441 G Street, NW
Washington, DC 20548

Dear Mr. Goldstein:

Thank you for the opportunity to review and comment on the Government Accountability Office's (GAO) draft Report entitled *Regulatory Fee Process Needs To Be Updated* (GAO-12-686) concerning the assessment and collection of annual regulatory fees from the entities regulated by the Federal Communications Commission (FCC or Commission).[1] The Commission is responsible for implementing Congress' directives in section 9 of the Communications Act of 1934, as amended,[2] and the draft Report contains thoughtful analyses and proposals regarding our implementation of the statute. We are pleased to have this opportunity to review and comment on it.

After describing the study and its conclusions, the GAO makes three specific recommendations on how the FCC could improve its administration of the regulatory fee process.[3] These recommendations are addressed in a pending Notice of Proposed Rulemaking on Regulatory Fee Reform (*Fee Reform NPRM*).[4] The *Fee Reform NPRM* sets forth three goals to guide the Commission in its reform initiative: fairness, administrability, and sustainability. To achieve these goals the Commission proposes a series of fundamental changes to its regulatory fee program that include, but are not limited to, proposals contained in the draft Report's recommendations.

The GAO first recommends that the Commission determine whether and how the current schedule of regulatory fees should be revised to reflect the current telecommunications industry and the Commission's regulatory activities. The GAO states that this reevaluation should include an overall analysis of the appropriate number of individual fee categories and the bases on which fees are calculated. The GAO further states that the Commission should consider in its analysis the processes of other agencies that are funded by regulatory fees and, if appropriate, propose legislation needed to implement any needed changes to the FCC's current statutory authority.

The GAO's second recommendation is that the Commission recalculate the full-time equivalent number of employees(FTEs) assigned to each fee category and establish a process to assure that this analysis is performed at least biennially, consistent with general federal guidance

---

[1] Government Accountability Office, *Regulatory Fee Process Needs to be Updated*, GAO 12-686 (Aug. 2012) (GAO draft Report or draft Report).

[2] 47 U.S.C. § 159.

[3] GAO draft Report at 37.

[4] *In the Matter of Procedures for Assessment and Collection of Regulatory Fees*, MD Docket No. 12-201, FCC 12-77, July 13, 2012. We have attached a copy of the *Fee Reform NPRM* for your reference.

on user fees.[5] The GAO's third and final recommendation is that the Commission increase the transparency of its regulatory fee process by describing in each future year's NPRM and subsequent order the methodology and analysis used to allocate between fees among fee categories and by providing additional information on the year in which any cited FTE data was collected, the effect of any other adjustments made to the fees, and the amount of excess fees collected in previous years

Consistent with the Commission's goals of fairness and administrability and with the GAO's recommendations, the *Fee Reform NPRM* seeks comment on replacing the Fiscal Year (FY) 1998 FTE data now used to calculate regulatory fees with updated FY 2012 FTE data. Interested parties are also asked to address the related issues of how to assure that any resulting reallocation of FTEs within and among the FCC's bureaus is fair and equitable, and how the Commission might mitigate any significant increase in regulatory fees that may result from such reallocations. The *Fee Reform NPRM* also seeks comment on whether reducing the number of regulatory fee categories would be advisable, and whether new fee categories should be created for new telecommunications services like broadband. Interested parties are also asked to address whether the different bases on which regulatory fees are currently calculated (for example, numbers of subscribers, size of market served, or revenues) should be reduced or made uniform among all services. Consistent with the GAO's recommendation that the Commission consider the processes of other regulatory fee-funded agencies in evaluating its own proposed reforms, we will place a copy of the GAO's final Report in the record of the rulemaking so that interested parties may comment on the Report's recommendations and analyses.

Transparency is an essential element of fairness and administrability. In line with the GAO's recommendations on enhanced disclosure of information on our cost allocation methodology and the amount of fees it produces, the Commission plans to implement this recommendation, and as many other reforms as possible, in the next annual (FY 2013) regulatory fee proceeding.

Finally, in order to assure the sustainability of the reforms adopted in this proceeding, the *Fee Reform NPRM* seeks comment on how to assure that fees remain accurately calibrated to reflect the dynamism and convergence in the telecommunications industry and will be equitably distributed among regulatees. Consistent with the GAO's specific recommendation that the FCC review its FTE allocations at least biennially, the *Fee Reform NPRM* seeks comment on the frequency with which the Commission should revisit its allocations, specifically asking whether this reexamination should be undertaken at regular intervals, such as annually, or in response to comments by fee payors in the context of the annual regulatory fee collection NPRM. As to the GAO's recommendation regarding changes to the Commission's current statutory authority, should Congress decide to address these issues, the Commission stands ready to provide whatever information Congress may request.

Finally, the GAO proposes that Congress consider whether any excess regulatory fee collections should be appropriated for the Commission's use, or, if not, what the disposition of these funds should be. The GAO also suggests that Congress consider amending the Commission's annual appropriations language to permit reconciliation of excess collections or to otherwise specify how the Commission is to handle any future excess collections. Should Congress decide to examine these issues, or any other issues regarding regulatory fees, the Commission will of course provide whatever information Congress may request.

---

[5] GAO Draft Report at 37.

2

The fact that the regulatory fee reform proposals embodied in the GAO's three recommendations dovetail so completely with the objectives and proposals in the Commission's *Fee Reform NPRM* demonstrates consensus on the need for reform and important issues that must be carefully considered in achieving it. We are grateful to the GAO for its contribution to this effort and appreciate the opportunity to comment on the draft Report.

Sincerely,

David Robbins
Managing Director

Attachment

3

# Appendix III: GAO Contact and Staff Acknowledgments

| | |
|---|---|
| **GAO Contact** | Mark L. Goldstein, (202) 512-2834 or goldsteinm@gao.gov |
| **Staff Acknowledgments** | In addition to the contact above, Tammy Conquest (Assistant Director), Juan P. Avila, Russell Burnett, Patrick Dudley, Fred Evans, Colin Fallon, Bob Homan, Bert Japikse, Jacqueline M. Nowicki, Joshua Ormond, Steve Rabinowitz, and Alwynne Wilbur made key contributions to this report. |